Switch
It On

Contents

What Is Light? 4

Light Up the Night 6

The Light of Life 8

The Color Spectrum 10

The Electromagnetic Spectrum 11

Good Vibrations 12

Listening In 14

Turn It Down! 16

Light and Sound 18

A Shocking Discovery 20

The Power of Magnets 22

Modern Power Plants 24

Simple Circuits 26

Just Switch It On! 28

Glossary 30

Index 31

Discussion Starters 32

Features

We all know that the sun is bright, but just how bright is it? Find out on page 6.

What in the world is a decibel? Check out page 17 for more information.

A man with a kite in a thunderstorm showed that lightning is electricity. Read page 21 to find out who this man was and what he did.

Make your own simple circuit and discover the best materials for conducting electricity. Just follow the instructions on page 27.

What makes a rainbow?

Visit **www.rigbyinfoquest.com**
for more about **LIGHT.**

What Is Light?

Light is energy that we can see. Nearly all the light we use comes from our own star, the sun. We are able to see objects because the sun's light **reflects** off them. Many people used to think that the moon was a source of light. We now know that what we see when we look at the moon is really the reflected light of the sun.

There is no air in space, but the sun's light travels through empty space to reach Earth. It travels that distance in about four minutes.

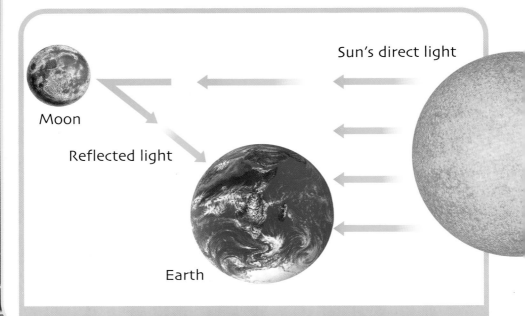

Sun's direct light

Moon

Reflected light

Earth

Nothing travels faster than the speed of light.

Even when the sun sets, we are not always in darkness because there is often reflected light from the moon.

Light Up the Night

People have always needed to see what they were doing and where they were going. People first used fire to light up their surroundings at night. However, when they moved away from the fire, they were in the dark again.

People needed a way to carry light and to have it whenever they wanted it. Candles and oil lamps helped, but it was not until Thomas Edison invented the electric lightbulb in 1879 that people finally had a dependable source of light.

The brightness of sunlight at noon is over 300 times stronger than the average lightbulb.

Tungsten wire

Inside a lightbulb, there
is a very thin wire made
of a metal called tungsten.
When an electric current
passes through this wire,
it gets very hot. This causes
the wire to glow brightly.

The Light of Life

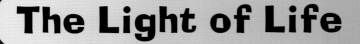

Almost all living things need light to stay alive. Plants need light to grow, reproduce, and create the oxygen we breathe. Without natural sunlight and the heat it carries, life as we know it would end.

Sunlight also affects us in other ways. We often feel happier on a sunny day. People like to go on vacation to sunny places. Sunlight—or a lack of it—even helps us feel when we should go to sleep and when we should wake up!

Is It Night or Day?

During a solar eclipse, the moon moves between Earth and the sun. If you are in the moon's shadow, the sun's light is blocked. The sky gets dark during the day!

Solar Eclipse

Sun   Moon   Earth

 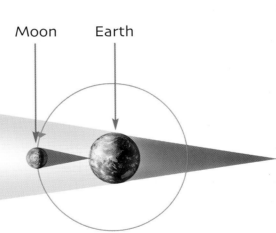

SITESEEING · SCIENCE & TECHNOLOGY

What makes a rainbow?

Visit www.rigbyinfoquest.com
for more about LIGHT.

The Color Spectrum

The colors in sunlight are red, orange, yellow, green, blue, indigo, and violet. We see these colors in a rainbow. These colors make up the color **spectrum** of visible light.

We see colors of objects because they reflect different colors of the spectrum. When you see a green apple, you are actually seeing the light from the green part of the spectrum reflected. The rest of the light goes into the apple. White objects reflect all the colors. Black objects take in all the light. So black isn't really a color at all!

This pepper reflects red light and takes in, or absorbs, the other colors.

The Electromagnetic Spectrum

Visible light is only one part of the **electromagnetic** spectrum of energy waves. Gamma rays, the shortest waves, have the most energy.

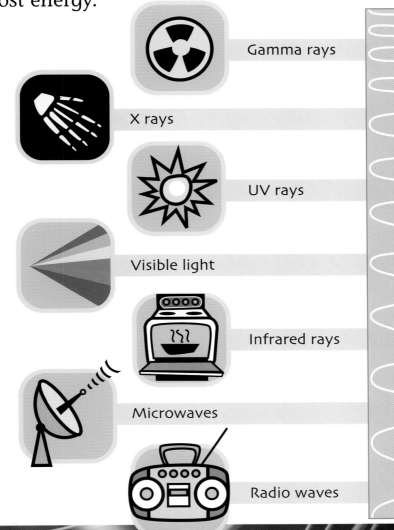

Gamma rays

X rays

UV rays

Visible light

Infrared rays

Microwaves

Radio waves

Good Vibrations

Objects shake, or vibrate, the air around them when they move. This vibration creates waves that travel in all directions, like the ripples that are made when a stone is dropped in a pool of water. When these waves reach our ears, we sense them as sound.

Sound travels through air, water, and some solids. Sound cannot travel where there is no atmosphere. That's why outer space is a silent place.

The sounds we hear from flying insects or birds are the vibrations made by the rapid movement of their wings.

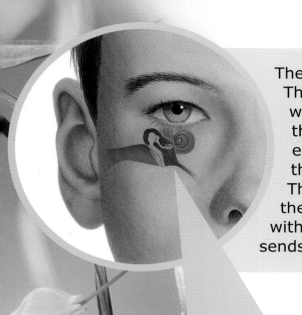

The ear has three parts. The outer ear collects sound waves and directs them to the middle ear. The middle ear vibrates and makes the sound waves louder. The sound waves then reach the inner ear, which is filled with liquid. This vibrates and sends messages to the brain.

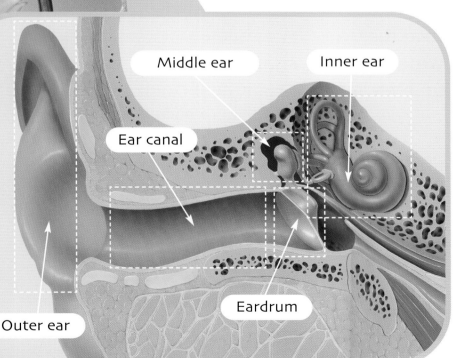

Middle ear

Inner ear

Ear canal

Outer ear

Eardrum

Listening In

Have you ever wondered how you can switch on a radio and hear your favorite song? Radio stations use transmitters to send out electromagnetic waves. These radio waves are received by the antenna on your radio. Your radio turns the signal into sound waves you can hear.

Every radio station uses a different **frequency**. When you turn the tuner on your radio, you're actually changing the frequencies your radio will catch.

The radio station sends sounds as electrical signals to a radio transmitter.

The radio transmitter sends the radio waves across the country.

Who's Calling?

When someone speaks into a telephone, the sound vibrates the phone's **diaphragm** and creates an electrical signal. This signal travels along a telephone line. It is converted back into sound waves by another diaphragm in your phone's earpiece. Cell phones use radio waves to send the signal.

Your radio is tuned to these waves. The radio speaker turns the waves back into sound.

Turn It Down!

Hearing is one of our most important senses, but we don't all like the same sounds. Sounds that people don't like are often called noise. Some noises, such as car horns and train whistles, are very important because they warn us of possible dangers.

If sounds are too loud, they can harm your ears. You can guard your ears by wearing ear protectors around noisy equipment and by making sure your music is not turned up too loud.

WORD BUILDER

Sound is measured in units called decibels. A bel is also a unit of sound, but it is hardly ever used. One bel is equal to ten decibels.

Decibels

Drum — 150

160

140

Sound at this level can hurt your ears. → 130

120

Power tools — 110

100

90

80

Telephone —

70

60

Washing machine — 50

40

30

20

Quiet living room — 10

0

17

Light and Sound

Have you ever heard the sound of a jet overhead and then been surprised when you looked up because it was not where you expected it to be? This happens because sound travels very slowly. Light travels at about 186,000 miles per second through the air. Sound, however, travels at only about 0.2 of a mile per second.

When you look up at the jet, you see where it is now. The sound comes from where the jet was when the sound started traveling.

You can tell how far away a storm is by counting the seconds between seeing a lightning flash and hearing the thunder. Every five seconds is about one mile. Using this method, you can tell if a storm is coming closer or moving away.

Concordes and some other jets can fly faster than the speed of sound.

A Shocking Discovery

Through time, people have known that a special force existed. This force is caused by electricity. Until about 400 years ago, the source of this force and how it worked were mysteries.

As long as 2,400 years ago, the Greeks noticed that rubbing fur against amber would make the amber attract small, lightweight things such as hair. This force is caused by **static electricity.** You can make static electricity by rubbing your hair with a balloon. Watch what happens to your hair!

Benjamin Franklin (1706–1790)

Benjamin Franklin proved that lightning is electricity by flying a kite in the middle of a thunderstorm! He had attached an iron spike to the kite and an iron key to the end of the kite string he was holding. When lightning struck the iron spike, a spark traveled from the key to his hand.

Do not try this yourself! Benjamin Franklin was very lucky—he could have been killed by the electricity!

The Power of Magnets

Magnets and electricity are very closely related. Magnets can be used to create electricity, and electricity can be used to create magnets. When a magnet is moved through a coil of wire, it produces an electric current. This is how electric **generators** work. We use electric currents to power our lights and televisions.

When an electric current flows along a wire, it produces a **magnetic field.** This allows people to make powerful electromagnets that can be switched on and off.

A Simple Electromagnet

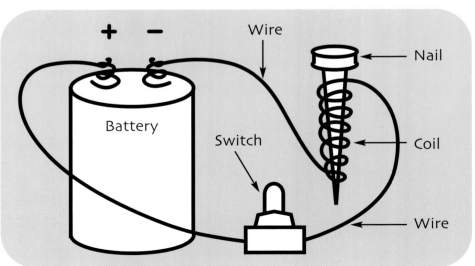

+   -

Wire

Nail

Battery

Switch

Coil

Wire

This crane uses an electromagnet to pick up a metal carton. The crane operator switches the electromagnet on to lift the load and then switches it off to let the load go.

Modern Power Plants

Modern power plants use large generators to produce electricity. Generators produce electricity when they are turned by a machine called a **turbine.** Turbines can be turned by various forces. Hydroelectric power plants use the force of falling water as a source of power for a turbine.

A Hydroelectric Power Plant

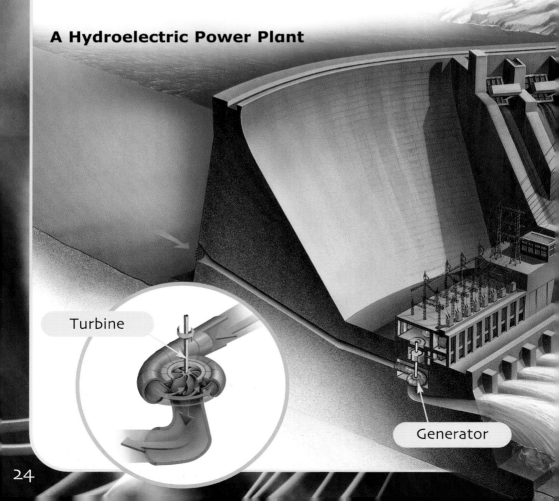

Turbine

Generator

In many places, coal, oil, or gas are burned to heat water and produce steam that turns the turbine. Sometimes nuclear reactors are used to heat the water. Windmills, or wind turbines, use the force of the wind to produce electricity.

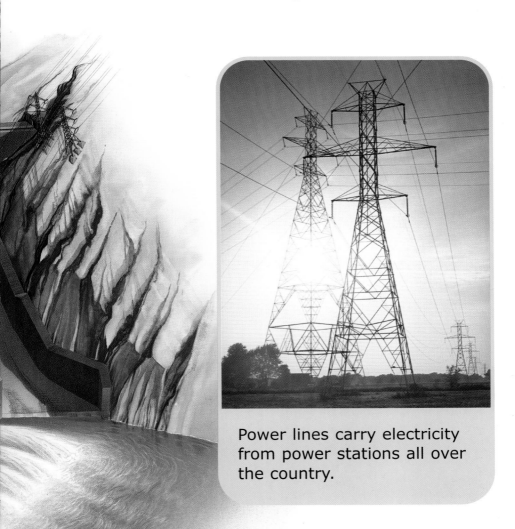

Power lines carry electricity from power stations all over the country.

Simple Circuits

When we use a light switch or turn on a television, we are actually completing a loop called an electrical circuit. When a switch is turned on, it completes the loop and an electric current can flow. When the switch is turned off, it breaks the loop.

Electricity travels through some materials better than others. Materials that allow electricity to travel easily are called good conductors. Good conductors include metals such as copper, gold, and iron.

A Simple Circuit

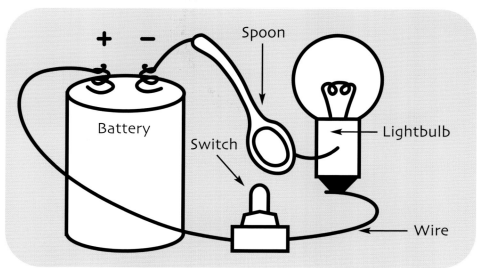

+ −

Spoon

Battery

Switch

Lightbulb

Wire

You can make your own circuit and test different materials to see how well they conduct electricity.

You will need:

- a battery
- 4 pieces of wire
- 1 bulb
- 4 alligator clips
- a switch
- everyday objects, such as a spoon, pencil, eraser, and key

Procedure:

1) Connect the circuit to match the diagram on page 26. Connect the two alligator clips to a metal object, like a spoon, as in the picture. When you turn on the switch, the bulb should light up.

2) Take the two alligator clips off the spoon and attach them to the ends of another object. If the bulb is still bright, this object is a good conductor. If the bulb doesn't light up, the object is a poor conductor of electricity. Try different objects and see what happens.

Just Switch It On!

It wasn't until about eighty years ago that sound and light were combined to provide us with information and entertainment. Before then, silent movies provided pictures but no sound. Radio provided sound but no pictures.

Today, modern inventions such as television and home computers offer both sight and sound as soon as we switch them on. Experiments in virtual reality are pushing what can be offered even further. Someday, we may even be able to smell, taste, and feel images beamed into our houses.

Outdoor concerts often include light shows.

Glossary

diaphragm – a thin piece of stretched material which is vibrated by sound

electromagnetic – a word describing the force that combines electricity and magnetism. Electromagnetic waves of energy include light waves, heat waves, and radio waves.

frequency – the number of peaks per second in a wave, such as a radio wave sent out by a radio signal

generator – a machine that produces electricity by turning a magnet inside a coil of wire

magnetic field – the area around a magnet or electric coil where metals are pulled in by magnetic force

reflect – to bounce off a surface

spectrum – a broad range of related things, such as the colors of the rainbow

static electricity – electricity that builds up in an object and stays there. You can see the effects of static electricity by rubbing a balloon against your hair.

turbine – a machine driven by water, wind, gas, or steam that turns a generator

Index

Diaphragm

color spectrum	10
Edison, Thomas	6
electricity	6–7, 14-15, 20–22, 24–27
electromagnetic spectrum	11
electromagnets	22–23
Franklin, Benjamin	21
generators	22, 24
light	4–11, 18, 28
magnets	22
moon	4–5, 9
radio	14–15, 28
solar eclipses	9
sound	12–19, 28
sun	4–6, 8–9
telephones	15, 17
turbines	24–25

Discussion Starters

1 Sight, hearing, and touch help us to understand the world around us. Which of these three senses do you think is the most important? If you had to be without one of these senses, which one would you choose? The senses work together. Can you think of some examples?

2 Imagine life without electricity. Make a list of ten things in your home or classroom that use electricity. Which of these things would you miss the most? Why?

3 What is the difference between sound and noise? Can you think of some sounds you like that other people think are just noise? Why don't you agree?